Other Books by Marge Piercy

Fiction

GOING DOWN FAST
DANCE THE EAGLE TO SLEEP
SMALL CHANGES
WOMAN ON THE EDGE OF TIME
THE HIGH COST OF LIVING
VIDA

Poetry

BREAKING CAMP
HARD LOVING
4-TELLING (*with Bob Hershon, Emmett Jarrett, and Dick Lourie*)
TO BE OF USE
LIVING IN THE OPEN
THE TWELVE-SPOKED WHEEL FLASHING

Play

THE LAST WHITE CLASS (*with Ira Wood*)

The Moon Is Always Female

THE MOON

IS ALWAYS FEMALE

by Marge Piercy

ALFRED A. KNOPF   New York   1985

THIS IS A BORZOI BOOK
PUBLISHED BY ALFRED A. KNOPF, INC.

Brush and ink drawing of cat from "Studies of Flowers and
Animals" by Shen Chou, 1494, Ming Dynasty. Collection of the
National Palace Museum, Taipei, Taiwan, the Republic of China.

Grateful acknowledgment is made to the following periodicals, where
most of these poems previously appeared:

*The Ark, Aspect, Blue Buildings, Cedar Rock, Chrysalis, Croton Review,
Gallimaufry, The Guardian, Hampden-Sydney Poetry Review, Hard
Pressed, Hudson River Anthology, Lady Unique, The Little Magazine,
The Lunar Calendar, Mississippi Mud, Moon Dance, Mosaic, Mother
Jones, National Forum, Open Places, Paintbrush, Painted Bridge
Quarterly, Poetry Now, Poets On, Pulp, Pushcart Press, Real Paper,
Shankpainter, Sister Courage, Sojourner, The Spirit That Moves Us,
Tendril, The Thirteenth Moon, Transatlantic Review, waves,
Woman Poet.*

Library of Congress Cataloging in Publication Data
Piercy, Marge.   The moon is always female.   I.   Title.
PS3566.I4M6   811'.5'4   79-21866
ISBN 0-394-50977-3   ISBN 0-394-73859-4 pbk.

Manufactured in the United States of America

Published April 30, 1980
Reprinted Six Times
Eighth Printing, April, 1985

For Woody

Contents

THE LUNAR CYCLE

HAND GAMES

The inside chance

Dance like a jackrabbit
in the dunegrass, dance
not for release, no
the ice holds hard but
for the promise. Yesterday
the chickadees sang *fever*,
fever, the mating song.
You can still cross ponds
leaving tracks in the snow
over the sleeping fish
but in the marsh the red
maples look red
again, their buds swelling.
Just one week ago a blizzard
roared for two days.
Ice weeps in the road.
Yet spring hides
in the snow. On the south
wall of the house
the first sharp crown
of crocus sticks out.
Spring lurks inside the hard
casing, and the bud
begins to crack. What seems
dead pares its hunger
sharp and stirs groaning.
If we have not stopped
wanting in the long dark,

we will grasp our desires
soon by the nape.
Inside the fallen brown
apple the seed is alive.
Freeze and thaw, freeze
and thaw, the sap leaps
in the maple under the bark
and although they have
pronounced us dead, we
rise again invisibly,
we rise and the sun sings
in us sweet and smoky
as the blood of the maple
that will open its leaves
like thousands of waving hands.

When a friend dies

When a friend dies
the salmon run no fatter.
The wheat harvest will feed no more bellies.
Nothing is won by endurance
but endurance.
A hunger sucks at the mind
for gone color after the last bronze
chrysanthemum is withered by frost.
A hunger drains the day,
a homely sore gap
after a tooth is pulled,
a red giant gone nova,
an empty place in the sky
sliding down the arch
after Orion in night as wide
as a sleepless staring eye.
When pain and fatigue wrestle
fatigue wins. The eye shuts.
Then the pain rises again at dawn.
At first you can stare at it.
Then it blinds you.

Night flight

Vol de nuit: It's that French
phrase comes to me out of a dead
era, a closet where the bones of pets
and dried jellyfish are stored. Dreams
of a twenty-year-old are salty water
and the residual stickiness of berry jam
but they have the power to paralyze
a swimmer out beyond her depth and strength.
Memory's a minefield.

Saint Exupéry was a favorite of my French
former husband. Every love has its
season, its cultural artifacts, shreds
of popular song like a billboard
peeling in strips to the faces behind,
endearments and scents, patchouli,
musk, cabbage, vanilla, male cat, smoked
herring. Yet I call this cobalt and crystal
outing, vol de nuit.

Alone in a row on the half empty late
plane I sit by the window holding myself.
As the engines roar and the plane quivers
and then bursts forward I am tensed
and tuned for the high arc of flight
between snowfields, frozen lakes and the cold
distant fires of the clustered stars. Below
the lights of cities burn like fallen galaxies,
ordered, radial, pulsing.

Sometimes hurtling down a highway through
the narrow cone of headlights I feel
moments of exaltation, but my night
vision is poor. I pretend at control
as I drive, nervously edging that knowledge
I am not really managing. I am in the hands
of strangers and of luck. By flight *he* meant
flying and I mean being flown, totally
beyond volition, willfully.

We fall in love with strangers whose faces
radiate a familiar power that reminds us
of something lost before we had it.
The braille of the studious fingers instructs
exactly what we have succumbed to, far too late
to close, to retract the self that has extruded
from us naked, vulnerable and sticky,
the foot, the tentative eyestalked head
of the mating snail.

To fall in love so late is dangerous. Below,
lights are winking out. Cars crawl into driveways
and fade into the snow. Planes make me think
of dying suddenly, and loving of dying
slowly, the heat loss of failure and betrayed
trust. Yet I cast myself on you, closing
my eyes as I leap and then opening them wide
as I land. Love is plunging into darkness toward
a place that may exist.

Arriving

People often labor to attain
what turns out to be entrance
to a small closet
or a deep pit
or sorrow like a toothache of the brain.

I wanted you. I fought you
for yourself, I wrestled
to open you, I hung on.
I sat on my love as on the lid
of a chest holding a hungry bear.
You were what I wanted: you
still are. Now my wanting
feeds on success and grows,
a cowbird chick in a warbler's
nest, bigger by the hour, bolder
and louder, screeching and gaping
for more, flapping bald wings.

I am ungainly in love as a house
dancing. I am a factory chimney
that has learned to play Bach
like a carillon. I belch rusty
smoke and flames and strange music.
I am a locomotive that wants
to fly to the moon.

I should wear black
on black like a Greek village woman,
making signs against the evil eye
and powder my head white. Though I try
to hide it I burn with joy like a bonfire
on a mountain, and tomorrow
and the next day make me shudder
equally with hope and fear.

Excursions, incursions

1.

"Learning to manage the process
of technological innovation
more productively" is the theme
of the speech the man beside me
on the plane to Washington
will be saying to a Congressional
subcommittee. He works at M.I.T.
He drinks a martini, glancing sideways.
His watch flashes numbers; it houses
a tiny computer. He observes
me in snatches, data to analyze:
the two-piece V-neck dress
from New York, the manuscript
I am cutting, the wild black
hair, the dirt under my stubby nails.
It doesn't scan. I pretend
I do not see him looking
while I try to read his speech,
pretending not to: a neutron
bomb of deadly language that kills
all warm-blooded creatures
but leaves the system standing.
He rates my face and body at-
tractive but the presence
disturbing. Chop, chop, I want
to say, sure, we are enemies.
Watch out. I try to decide
if I can learn anything useful
to my side if I let him

engage me in a game of
conversation.

2.

At the big round table in the university
club, the faculty are chatting
about wives, marriages, divorces, visiting
arrangements. They all belong
to the same kinship system. They have
one partner at a time, then terminate.
Monogamy means that the husband has
sex only a couple of times with each
other female, I figure out, and
the wife, only with him. Afterwards
the children spend summers/weekends/
Sundays with the father.

Listening becomes eavesdropping and they
begin to feel my silence like a horse
in the diningroom. Gradually as I sit
my hair mats. Feathers stick up from
it, crow and eagle. My cheeks break
out into painted zigzag designs. My spear
leans against the back of my chair.
They begin to question me, oh, um,
do you live communally? What do
you mean, "open"? Hair breaks through
the back of my hands. My fangs
drum on the table top. In another moment

I will swing by my long prehensile
tail from the crystal chandelier,
shitting in the soup.

3.

The men are laughing as I approach
and then they price me: that calculating
scan. Everything turns into hornets
buzzing, swarming. One will
tell me about his wife
weeping tears of pure beersuds;
one is even now swaggering down
the Tombstone set of his mind, the fastest
gun; one will let me know in the next
half hour he thinks political writers
are opportunistic simpletons, and women
have minds of goat fudge; one will
only try unceasingly to bed me as if
I were the week's prize, and he wears
a chain of fellowships and grants
like sharpshooters' medals. Mostly they
will chase the students and drink, mostly
they will gossip and put each other
down, mostly they will complain. I
am here for the women, a political
task. They think they have a label
for that. I am on vacation from sex
and love, from the fatty broth
of my life. I am seeking to be useful,

the good godmother. We are acting
in different fables. I know the plots
of theirs, but none of them recognize
mine, except the students, who understand
at once they will be allowed
to chew me to the bones.

4.

I am sitting on a kitchen chair.
My feet do not reach the floor.
If I sit forward, they'll rest on
a rung, but if I do that, the women
will stop talking and look at me
and I'll be made to go outside
and "play" in this taffeta dress.
What they say is not what they
are talking about, which lumps
just underneath. If I listen, if I
screw up my face and hold my breath
and listen, I'll see it, the moving
bump under the rug, that snake in the
tablecloth jungle, the bulge
in women's dresses you aren't supposed
to notice. I listen and listen
but it doesn't go anyplace,
nobody comes out all
right in the end. I get bored
and kick the table leg and am sent
outside to sulk, still not knowing

why everybody said Uncle looked
like he was asleep when he had
lipstick on, in the funny box.

I never got there, into the hot
wet heart of the kitchen gossip,
to sit twisting the ring on my finger
worn smooth, saying my hubby, my old
man, *him*. I never grew up, Mama,
I grew off, I grew outside. I grew
like crazy. I am the calico
mouse gnawing at the foundations.
The sweet snake is my friend who chews
on the roots of the hangman's tree
to bring it down. I am the lump
under the tablecloth that moves
stealthily toward the cream pitcher.
After years under the rug like a tumor
they invite me into the parlor, Mama,
they pay me by check and it doesn't bounce.
I'm giving a speech tonight. Do they
think I'm kidding? The walls I write
on are for sale now, but the message
is the same as I wrote in
blood on the jail house wall.
Energy flowing through me gets turned
into money and they take that back,
but the work remains, Mama, under
the carpet, in the walls, out
in the open. It goes on talking
after they've shut me up.

Dirty poem

Snow lies on my fields
though the air is so warm I want
to roll on my back and wriggle.
Sure, the dark downhill weep shows
who's winning, and the thatch of tall
grass is sticking out of the banks,
but I want to start digging and planting.
My swelling hills, my leafbrown loamy
soil interlaced with worms red as mouths,
my garden,

        why don't you hurry up
and take your clothes off?

Leonard Avenue

Two floors down I loll
in warm cinnamon-scented water.
Box piled on box on box,
up under the eaves you float
in turgid bloodwarm sleep.
Bundled in my robe I climb
bearing coffee steaming incense
on the chill stairway air.
We'll drink it dabbling in bed
on the shore between waking and sleep
where you enter my wetness and I
take in your warmth.

Limited but fertile possibilities
are offered by this brochure

We cannot have monogrammed towels
or matches with our names on. We cannot
have children. We cannot share joint
tax returns. We don't have a past.
Our future is a striped unicorn, fragile,
shy, the first of a new
species born without kind
to hostile kin. We can work together
snarling and giggling and grunting.
Every few years we can have a play
as offspring. We can travel. We can
go away and come back. We can shake
each other rattling honest. We can have long
twining soft voiced phonecalls that leave me
molten and fevered. We can make each other
laugh, cry, groan till our flesh shines
phosphorescent, till heat shimmers in the room,
till we steam with joy and streamers of light
run down the insides of our eyes.
We can love. We can love. We can
love.

Intruding

What are you doing up, my cat
complains as I come into the living
room at two in the morning: she
is making eyes through the glass
at a squat ruffed grey tom. He fades
back, only the gold eyes shining
like headlights under the bird feeder.

Retreat with all deliberate speed
says the skunk in the path
at the marsh's edge, tail upraised
quivering in shape like a question
mark but in meaning an exclamation
point.

You are too near my nest so I will
let you believe you can catch and
eat me, says the whip-poor-will
leading me through the thorniest thickets
uphill and down ravines of briar
as it drags its apparently broken wing.

This is my lair, my home, my master,
my piss-post, my good brown blanket,
my feeding dish, my bone farm, all
mine and my teeth are long and sharp

as icicles and my tongue is red as your
blood I will spill if you do not
run, the German shepherd says loudly
and for half a block.

In the center of her web the spider
crouches to charge me. In the woods
the blue jay shrieks and the squirrels
perch over my head chittering while all
the small birds bide silent in the leaves.
Wherever I march on two legs
I am walking on somebody's roof.

But when I sit still and alone
trees hatch warblers rapid as sparks.
The price of seeing is silence.
A voracious furnace of shrew darts
in the grass like a truncated snake.
On my arm a woodnymph lights probing
me curiously, faintly, as she opens
and closes the tapestried doors of flight.

The damn cast

It's a barracuda, you say,
that attacked, swallowed your leg
and choked to death, still
attached. It's moby prick,
the plaster caster's bone-dry dream.
It's a Beef Wellington with your thigh
as tenderloin; or a two foot
long red-hot getting stale in the bun.

You can no longer sneak from behind
to tickle or seize. For ten minutes
I hear you thumping up the staircase,
a dinosaur in lead boots,
before you collapse carefully in the chair
face red as borscht and puffing steam.

We find a freemasonry of the temporarily
halt: people with arms in slings,
men limping on canes, women
swinging on crutches, cross the street
to ask your story, tell theirs. But
the permanently disabled whiz by

in their wheelchairs indifferent.
They know you only visit
at difficulty. By spring you'll
be running up my stairs two
at a time, and you won't remember
the mountain that loomed in each building,
the heavy doors fortressed against you.

All of you I can still touch,
I cherish: how easily torn, how
quickly smashed we are. Each street
bristles with impaling machines.
I say, *Take Care*; yet we can't
love in armor, can't dance inside tanks,
can't wave at the world from a barnacle
shell. The same nerves that melt
us to butterscotch brandy sundaes
scream pain hot as laser drills.
Inside that long egg, you atrophy.

The wrong anger

Infighting, gut battles we all
wage so well. Carnage in the fish tank.
Alligators wrestling in bed.
Nuclear attack
across the breakfast table.
Duels in the women's center.
The fractioning faction fight.

Where does the bank president
drink his martinis? Where
do those who squeeze the juice
from the land till it blows
red dust in your eye
hang out on Saturday night?

It's easy to kick my dog,
my child, my lover, the woman
across the desk. People
burning their lives away
for pennies pile up in neighborhoods
like rusting car bodies.
Why not stroll down to the corner
yacht club and invite the chairman
of the board of I.T. & T.
to settle it with his fists?

How hard to war against those
too powerful to show us faces
of billboard lions smiling
from bloodflecked jaws. Their eyes
flick over us like letters
written too small to read,
streets seen from seven miles
up as they spread the peacock
tail of executive jets
across skies yellow with greed.
Their ashes rain down
on our scarred arms, the fall
out from explosions
they order by memo.

The cast off

This is a day to celebrate can-
openers, those lantern-jawed long-tailed
humping tools that cut through what keeps
us from what we need : a can of beans
trapped in its armor taunts the nails
and teeth of a hungry woman.

Today let us hear hurrahs for zippers,
those small shark teeth that part
politely to let us at what we want ;
the tape on packages that unlock
us birthday presents ; envelopes
we slit to thaw the frozen
words on the tundra of paper.

Today let us praise the small
rebirths, the emerging groundhog
from the sodden burrow ; the nut
picked from the broken fortress of walnut
shell, itself pried from the oily fruit
shaken from the high turreted
city of the tree.

Today let us honor the safe whose door
hangs ajar; the champagne bottle
with its cork bounced off the ceiling
and into the soup tureen; the Victorian lady
in love who has removed her hood, her cloak,
her laced boots, her stockings, her overdress,
her underdress, her wool petticoat, her linen
petticoats, her silk petticoats, her whalebone
corset, her bustle, her chemise, her drawers, and
who still wants to! Today let us praise the cast
that finally opens, slit neatly in two
like a dinosaur egg, and out at last
comes somewhat hairier, powdered in dead skin
but still beautiful, the lost for months
body of my love.

Waiting outside

All day you have been on my mind,
a seagull perched on an old wharf
piling by the steely grip of its claws,
shrieking when any other comes too near,
waiting for fish or what the tide brings,
shaking out its long white wings like laundry.

All day you have been on my mind,
a thrift store glamour hat that doesn't fit
with a perky veil scratching my cheek,
with a feather hanging down like a broken
tail tickling my neck, settling its
big dome over my ears muffling sounds.

All day you have been on my mind,
a beauty shop hair dryer blowing sirocco,
wind off the Sahara bearing bad
news and sand that stifles, roaring
through my head thrust in the lion's hot mouth,
a helmet that clamps me here to bake.

All day you have been on my mind,
a steam iron pressing the convolutions
from my cortex, ironing me flat. Worrying
cooks my cells feverish. I am irritable
with love boiling into anxiety, till I grow
furious with you, lying under the surgeon's knife.

Will we work together?

You wake in the early grey
morning in bed alone and curse
me, that I am only
sometimes there. But when
I am with you, I light
up the corners, I am bright
as a fireplace roaring
with love, every bone in my back
and my fingers is singing
like a tea kettle on the boil.
My heart wags me, a big dog
with a bigger tail. I am
a new coin printed with
your face. My body wears
sore before I can express
on yours the smallest part
of what moves me. Words
shred and splinter.
I want to make with you
some bold new thing
to stand in the marketplace,
the statue of a goddess
laughing, armed and wearing
flowers and feathers. Like sheep
of whose hair is made
blankets and coats, I want
to force from this fierce sturdy
rampant love some useful thing.

In memoriam
Walter and Lillian Lowenfels

Born into history:
going headfirst through a trapdoor
from heaven into a river
of boiling sewage: what we do
rushes on with cans and bottles.
The good die still ringing
to the nails with hope like a fever.

A friend said of another old man, his war
is over. She could not understand
why he is toted about like a talking
head to demonstrations, press
conferences, unpacked, propped up.
I said, his war is mine.
He wants to be useful as long as he
can want. He needs freedom to blow
through him seeking its hard way.
Struggle wears the bones thin
as it sings in them, but there is no pension,
no retirement fund for the guerrilla.

Alice Paul, old suffragette ailing
on a poverty ward, commands loyalty
I can't deliver my aunt. The French
feminists who use de Beauvoir's apartment
for abortions, are her children. Her best love
runs flickering in their veins
altering the faces carved on their genes.

Walter, Lillian, you were my parents too.
Poet, communist, anthologist, writer of letters

of protest to *The New York Times,* jailbird
in the ice age fifties for your politics,
you crowed with life, Walter, in a rustle
of misfiled Thermofaxed work of poets
fifty years younger, Black, Native American,
Quebecois, voices that swarmed in your windows,
a flight of varicolored warblers escaped singing
from the prisons of the world. You grew old
in your craft but never respectable.
A fresh anger for a new outrage quickened you.
You did not think Jara in the stadium in Chile
as they crushed the fingers then the hands
before they killed him to silence, hurt less
than your friends shot in Spain in '38.

You poured out neat history for aperitifs
to whet the hunger for dinner to come.
You heard new voices each morning and fell
in love catching enthusiasm like a viral fever.
You roared your old loves, preening, showing
off for Lillian and sister Nan, hacking up
a roasted chicken with a cleaver so the drumsticks
flew while the women pretended terror.

I miss you, old man. You never gave up.
Your death caught you still soldiering
in the war I too will never see finished.
Goodbye, Walter and Lillian, becoming history.

Under red Aries

I am impossible, I know it,
a fan with a clattering blade loose,
a car with no second gear.
I want you to love freely, I want
you to love richly and many
but I want your mouth to taste of me
and I want to walk in your dreams naked.

You are impossible, you know it,
holy March hairiness, my green
eyed monster, my luna-
tic. On the turning spit of the full moon
my period starts flooding down and you
toss awake. Sleeping with you then
is spending a night on an airport
runway. Something groaning
from the ends of the earth is always
coming down and something overloaded
is taking off in a wake of ashes.

We are impossible, everybody says it.
I could have babysat in bobbysox
and changed you. Platoons of men
have camped on my life bivouacking
in their war. Now, presumably both adults,

I am still trying to change you.
We are cut from the same cloth, you say,
and what material is that? A crazy quilt
of satin and sackcloth, of sandpaper
and chiffon, of velvet and chickenwire.

I love you from my bones out, impulses
rising far down in the molten core
deep as orgasm in the moist and fiery pit
beyond ego. I love you from the center
of my life pulsating like a storm on the sun
shooting out arms of fire with power
enough to run a world or scorch it.
We are partially meshed in each other
and partially we turn free. We are
hooked into others like a machine
that could actually move forward,
a vehicle of flesh that could bring us
and other loving travelers to a new land.

The ordinary gauntlet

In May when the first warm days
open like peonies, the coat,
the jacket stay home.
Then making my necessary
way through streets I am impaled
on shish-kabob stares,
slobbering invitations,
smutfires of violence.
The man who blocks my path,
the man who asks my price,
the man who grabs with fat
hands like sweating crabs.

I grimace, I trot.
Put on my ugliest clothes,
layer over sweltering layer.
Sprint scowling and still
they prance in ugly numbers.

I, red meat, cunt
on the hoof, trade
insult for insult,
balance fear on coiled rage.
I pretend to carry easy

on my belt a ray gun.
I flick my finger. A neat
beam licks the air.
The man lights up
in neon and goes out.
My fantasy leaves me still
spread on the meat rack
of their hate.

On the first warm day
let me shoot up twelve
feet tall. Or grow
a hide armored as an
alligator. Then I would
relish the mild air,
I would stroll, my jagged
fangs glinting in
a real broad smile.

The long death

for Wendy Teresa Simon (September 25, 1954–August 7, 1979)

Radiation is like oppression,
the average daily kind of subliminal toothache
you get almost used to, the stench
of chlorine in the water, of smog in the wind.

We comprehend the disasters of the moment,
the nursing home fire, the river in flood
pouring over the sandbag levee, the airplane
crash with fragments of burnt bodies
scattered among the hunks of twisted metal,
the grenade in the marketplace, the sinking ship.

But how to grasp a thing that does not
kill you today or tomorrow
but slowly from the inside in twenty years.
How to feel that a corporate or governmental
choice means we bear twisted genes and our
grandchildren will be stillborn if our
children are very lucky.

Slow death can not be photographed for the six
o'clock news. It's all statistical,
the gross national product or the prime
lending rate. Yet if our eyes saw
in the right spectrum, how it would shine,
lurid as magenta neon.

If we could smell radiation like seeping
gas, if we could sense it as heat, if we
could hear it as a low ominous roar

of the earth shifting, then we would not sit
and be poisoned while industry spokesmen
talk of acceptable millirems and .02
cancer per population thousand.

We acquiesce at murder so long as it is slow,
murder from asbestos dust, from tobacco,
from lead in the water, from sulphur in the air,
and fourteen years later statistics are printed
on the rise in leukemia among children.
We never see their faces. They never stand,
those poisoned children together in a courtyard,
and are gunned down by men in three-piece suits.

The shipyard workers who built nuclear
submarines, the soldiers who were marched
into the Nevada desert to be tested by the H-
bomb, the people who work in power plants,
they die quietly years after in hospital
wards and not on the evening news.

The soft spring rain floats down and the air
is perfumed with pine and earth. Seedlings
drink it in, robins sip it in puddles,

you run in it and feel clean and strong,
the spring rain blowing from the irradiated
cloud over the power plant.

Radiation is oppression, the daily average
kind, the kind you're almost used to
and live with as the years abrade you,
high blood pressure, ulcers, cramps, migraine,
a hacking cough: you take it inside
and it becomes pain and you say, not
They are killing me, but *I am sick now*.

A battle of wills disguised

You and I, are we in the same story?
Sometimes, never, on Tuesdays and Fridays?
I never ordered this Mama costume.
I don't want to be Joan Crawford: she dies
in the last reel, relinquishing all.
This is my movie too, you know. Why
is there a woman in it trying to kill me?
I thought this was a love story, but
of how much you and I both love you?

You and I, are we fighting the same war?
Then why do you lie on the telephone,
your voice fuzzy with the lint of guilt?
If the enemy is north, why do the guns
point at my house? Why do you study karate
instead of artillery and guerrilla warfare?
Two generals command the armies of their bodies,
feinting, withdrawing, attacking. If it's the same
war, are you sure we're fighting on the same side?

You and I, are we in the same relationship?
Then when you say what a good night we had why
do I writhe awake? Why do you explain how much
better things are getting as you race
out the door, leap the hedge and catch the last
train to the city? After a week you call
from the Coast to say how close you're feeling.
If this is a detective story I know who did it,
but who are the cops I can call? Just you. Just me.

Intimacy

Why does my life so often
feel like a slither of entrails
pouring from a wound in my belly?
With both my hands I grasp
my wet guts, trying to force
them back in.
                    Why does my life
so often feel like a wild
black lake under the midnight
thunder where I am drowning,
waves crashing over my face
as I try to breathe.
                    Why
does my life feel like a war
I am fighting alone? Why are
you fighting me? Why aren't
you with me? If I die this instant
will you be more content
with the morning news?
Will your coffee taste better?
I am not your fate. I am not your government.
I am not your FBI. I am not
even your mother, not your father
or your nightmare or your health.

I am not a fence, not a wall.
I am not the law or the actuarial tables
of your insurance broker. I am
a woman with my guts loose
in my hands, howling and it is not
because I committed hara-kiri.
I suggest either you cook me
or sew me back up. I suggest you walk
into my pain as into the breaking
waves of an ocean of blood, and either
we will both drown or we will
climb out together and walk away.

To have without holding

Learning to love differently is hard,
love with the hands wide open, love
with the doors banging on their hinges,
the cupboard unlocked, the wind
roaring and whimpering in the rooms
rustling the sheets and snapping the blinds
that thwack like rubber bands
in an open palm.

It hurts to love wide open
stretching the muscles that feel
as if they are made of wet plaster,
then of blunt knives, then
of sharp knives.

It hurts to thwart the reflexes
of grab, of clutch; to love and let
go again and again. It pesters to remember
the lover who is not in the bed,
to hold back what is owed to the work
that gutters like a candle in a cave
without air, to love consciously,
conscientiously, concretely, constructively.

I can't do it, you say it's killing
me, but you thrive, you glow
on the street like a neon raspberry,
You float and sail, a helium balloon
bright bachelor's button blue and bobbing
on the cold and hot winds of our breath,
as we make and unmake in passionate
diastole and systole the rhythm
of our unbound bonding, to have
and not to hold, to love
with minimized malice, hunger
and anger moment by moment balanced.

My mother's novel

Married academic woman ten
years younger holding that microphone
like a bazooka, forgive
me that I do some number of things
that you fantasize but frame
impossible. Understand:
I am my mother's daughter,
a small woman of large longings.

Energy hurled through her
confined and fierce as in a wind
tunnel. Born to a mean
harried poverty crosshatched
by spidery fears and fitfully
lit by the explosions
of politics, she married her way
at length into the solid workingclass:
a box of house, a car she could
not drive, a TV set kept turned
to the blare of football,
terrifying power tools, used wall
to wall carpeting protected
by scatter rugs.

Out of backyard posies
permitted to fringe
the proud hanky lawn
her imagination hummed
and made honey,
occasionally exploding
in mad queen swarms.

I am her only novel.
The plot is melodramatic,
hot lovers leap out of
thickets, it makes you cry
a lot, in between the revolutionary
heroics and making good
home-cooked soup.
Understand: I am my mother's
novel daughter: I
have my duty to perform.

The low road

What can they do
to you? Whatever they want.
They can set you up, they can
bust you, they can break
your fingers, they can
burn your brain with electricity,
blur you with drugs till you
can't walk, can't remember, they can
take your child, wall up
your lover. They can do anything
you can't stop them
from doing. How can you stop
them? Alone, you can fight,
you can refuse, you can
take what revenge you can
but they roll over you.

But two people fighting
back to back can cut through
a mob, a snake-dancing file
can break a cordon, an army
can meet an army.

Two people can keep each other
sane, can give support, conviction,
love, massage, hope, sex.
Three people are a delegation,

a committee, a wedge. With four
you can play bridge and start
an organization. With six
you can rent a whole house,
eat pie for dinner with no
seconds, and hold a fund raising party.
A dozen make a demonstration.
A hundred fill a hall.
A thousand have solidarity and your own newsletter;
ten thousand, power and your own paper;
a hundred thousand, your own media;
ten million, your own country.

It goes on one at a time,
it starts when you care
to act, it starts when you do
it again after they said no,
it starts when you say *We*
and know who you mean, and each
day you mean one more.

What it costs

Now it costs to say
I will survive, now when
my words coat my clenched
teeth with blood, now
when I have been yanked
off love like a diver
whose hose is cut.
I push against
the dizzying onslaught
of heavy dark water.
Up or down? While
the heart kicks
like a strangled rabbit
and the lungs buckle
like poor balloons:
I will survive.

I will lift the leaden
coffin lid of the surface
and thrust my face
into the air.
I will feel the sun's
rough tongue on my face.
Then I'll start swimming
toward the coast
that must somewhere
blur the horizon
with wheeling birds.

Season of hard wind

Sometimes we grind elbows clashing
like stripped gears. Our wills bang.
We spark, exposed wires spitting, scorched.

I wring the phone cord in my hands, trying
to suck wine from that cold umbilicus.
Your voice enters my ear like pebbles thrown.

My body parts for you shuddering and you
enter my spine and my dreams. All night
we climb mountains in each other's skull, arguing.

When I imagine losing you I see a continent
of ice and blasted rock, of glaciers blue
as skim milk, bank vaults of iceberg.

I see a land without soil, where nothing grows
but the slow cliffhigh thrust of the glaciers
and a meaningless cairn of skulls at the pole.

I would go on, like Scott who trudging alone
saw another plodding beside him as he starved
and froze, his double, his despair, his death.

Lonely, I am not alone, but my mind surrounds
me with demon whispers, skeptical ghosts.
I prefer to quarrel with those I truly love.

Hand games

Intent gets blocked by noise.
How often what we spoke
in the bathtub, weeping
water to water, what we framed
lying flat in bed to the spiked
night is not the letter that arrives,
the letter we thought we sent. We drive
toward each other on expressways
without exits. The telephone
turns our voices into codes,
then decodes the words falsely,
terms of an equation
that never balances, a scale
forever awry with its foot
stuck up lamely like a scream.

Drinking red wine from a sieve,
trying to catch love in words,
its strong brown river in flood
pours through our weak bones.
A kitten will chase the beam of a flash
light over the floor. We learn
some precious and powerful forces

can not be touched, and what
we touch plump and sweet
as a peach from the tree, a tomato
from the vine, sheds the name
as if we tried to write in pencil
on its warm and fragrant skin.

Mostly the television is on
and the washer is running and the kettle
shrieks it's boiling while the telephone
rings. Mostly we are worrying about
the fuel bill and how to pay the taxes
and whether the diet is working
when the moment of vulnerability
lights on the nose like a blue moth
and flitters away through clouds of mosquitoes
and the humid night. In the leaking
sieve of our bodies we carry
the blood of our love.

The doughty oaks

Oaks don't drop their leaves
as elms and lindens do.
They evolved no corky layer,
no special tricks.
They shut off the water.
Leaves hang on withering
tougher than leather.
Wind tears them loose.

Slowly they grow, white oaks
under the pitch pines,
tap roots plunging
deep, enormous carrots.
By the marsh they turn
twisting, writhing
aging into lichens, contorted
like the wind solidified.

In the spring how stubborn
how cautious
clutching their wallets tight.
Long after the maples,
the beeches have leafed out
they sleep in their ragged leaves.
Reluctantly in the buzz and hum
they raise velvet

antlers flushed red,
then flash silvery tassels.
At last vaulted
green chambers of summer.

Ponderous, when mature, as elephants,
in the storm they slam castle doors.
They all prepare to be great
grandfathers, in the meantime
dealing in cup and saucer acorns.

When frost crispens the morning,
they give up nothing willingly.
Always fighting the season,
conservative, mulish.
I find it easy to admire in trees
what depresses me in people.

Armed combat in a café

How easy for us to argue
shoving the ugly counters
of jargon across the table,
mah-jong tiles slapping,
the bang of ego on ego
feminist versus Marxist cant.

To feel alienated
is easy, to use words
to hold the self free,
clean from the taffy
of loving, from the wet
sticky hands of need.

We use our politics
as French papas put broken
bottles, jagged glass on top
of the walls of suburban
villas, so no prowler
can climb over.

What closeness remains
is that of samurai
in ritual sword dance
combat, each hoping to
behead the other and,
invulnerable and armored, escape.

Poetry festival lover

He reads his poem about you,
making sure everyone in town
knows you have been lovers
as if he published his own
tabloid with banner head
and passed it out at the door.

He kneels at your feet as you sit
a stuffed duck at autographings
and holds the hand others
wait to have sign their
purchased books.

Alone the last night he asks
favors (blurbs, readings,
your name on a folder) but
not your favor: he wants
the position but not the work.

His private parts lie quiet
and the public is all
he's hot to screw.
Avoid the poet who tells
his love loudly in public;
in private he counts his money.

Complaint
of the exhausted author

Pain turns on its dull red warning light
dim and steady in the dark.
My back clanks like an old coal furnace.
My brain is a cellar bin
empty except for desiccated spiders.
Even the mice have dropped their neat
tracks and shipped out.
Everything I have to burn
is burned and the house grows cold.

I remember real hunger,
the urgency, then the lassitude,
a hollow pain roaring like a distant sea
and through it all the sense
of the body cutting its losses
of the cells shutting down one by one
the lights going out.

That hunger was bone chip sharp.
Not simple, not of the bargaining flesh,
this hunger snivels and whines.
The quaking, tail low but wagging
cur of the heart
has desires that hide and abide,
a lion in yellow dog clothing
who will, who will be fed.

Don't think because I speak strong words
that I am always strong.
What moves through me moves

on and leaves me empty as a storm sewer
when the rains have gone.

My ribs squeal like a bad accordion.
Feed me, mother me. Coddle my fears.
Or I will go like a mole through the garden
chewing off roots for spite. I will crawl
into the rafters and become a leak
dripping on your chest in bed.

I will turn into a fat rheumatic yellow dog
who sprawls all day on the kitchen floor
in front of the stove in everybody's way,
and if you make me move
I will fix you with a baleful blind eye
and sigh and limp.

I will turn into a cough you can't get
rid of, or a fog bank
that broods on the house.
At night I will take my old form
and steal to the typewriter
to write damp querulous poems
like this one.
Feed me before it's too late.

For strong women

A strong woman is a woman who is straining.
A strong woman is a woman standing
on tiptoe and lifting a barbell
while trying to sing Boris Godunov.
A strong woman is a woman at work
cleaning out the cesspool of the ages,
and while she shovels, she talks about
how she doesn't mind crying, it opens
the ducts of the eyes, and throwing up
develops the stomach muscles, and
she goes on shoveling with tears
in her nose.

A strong woman is a woman in whose head
a voice is repeating, I told you so,
ugly, bad girl, bitch, nag, shrill, witch,
ballbuster, nobody will ever love you back,
why aren't you feminine, why aren't
you soft, why aren't you quiet, why
aren't you dead?

A strong woman is a woman determined
to do something others are determined
not be done. She is pushing up on the bottom
of a lead coffin lid. She is trying to raise
a manhole cover with her head, she is trying
to butt her way through a steel wall.
Her head hurts. People waiting for the hole
to be made say, hurry, you're so strong.

A strong woman is a woman bleeding
inside. A strong woman is a woman making
herself strong every morning while her teeth
loosen and her back throbs. Every baby,
a tooth, midwives used to say, and now
every battle a scar. A strong woman
is a mass of scar tissue that aches
when it rains and wounds that bleed
when you bump them and memories that get up
in the night and pace in boots to and fro.

A strong woman is a woman who craves love
like oxygen or she turns blue choking.
A strong woman is a woman who loves
strongly and weeps strongly and is strongly
terrified and has strong needs. A strong woman is strong
in words, in action, in connection, in feeling;
she is not strong as a stone but as a wolf
suckling her young. Strength is not in her, but she
enacts it as the wind fills a sail.

What comforts her is others loving
her equally for the strength and for the weakness
from which it issues, lightning from a cloud.
Lightning stuns. In rain, the clouds disperse.
Only water of connection remains,
flowing through us. Strong is what we make
each other. Until we are all strong together,
a strong woman is a woman strongly afraid.

Apologies

Moments
when I care about nothing
except an apple:
red as a maple tree
satin and speckled
tart and winy.

Moments
when body is all:
fast as an elevator
pulsing out waves of darkness
hot as the inner earth
molten and greedy.

Moments
when sky fills my head:
bluer than thought
cleaner than number
with a wind
fresh and sour
cold from the mouth of the sea.

Moments
of sinking my teeth
into now like a hungry fox:
never otherwise
am I so cruel;
never otherwise
so happy.

The fisherman's catalogue:
a found poem

Orvis nymphs: dark hendrickson,
leadwing coachman, pale evening dun.

Cream midge. Grizzly wulff hairwing fly.

Wet flies: hornberg, quill gordon, ginger quill.

Weighted nymphs: zug bug, hare's ear, Ted's stone fly.

Caddis pupa of great brown and speckled sedge.
Pale sulphur dun thorax dry fly, Rat Faced McDougal.
King's river caddis downwing fly.

Silver doctor, green highlander, dusty miller,
black dose, rusty rat, hairy Mary
and the salmon muddler. And the popping frog.

Rainy 4th

I am someone who boots myself from bed
when the alarm cracks my sleep. Spineless
as raw egg on the tilted slab of day
I ooze toward breakfast to be born.
I stagger to my desk on crutches of strong coffee.

How sensuous then are the mornings we do
not rise. This morning we curl embracing
while rain crawls over the roof like a thousand
scuttling fiddler crabs. Set off a
twenty-one tea kettle salute
for a rainy 4th with the parade and races
cancelled, our picnic chilling disconsolate
in five refrigerators. A sneaky hooray
for the uneven gallop of the drops,
for the steady splash of the drainpipe,
for the rushing of the leaves in green
whooshing wet bellows, for the teeming wind
that blows the house before it in full sail.

We are at sea together in the woods.
The air chill enough for the quilt, warm
and sweet as cocoa and coconut we make
love in the morning when there's never time.
Now time rains over us liquid and vast.
We talk facing, elastic parentheses.
We dawdle in green mazes of conversing

seeking no way out but only farther into
the undulating hedges, grey statues of nymphs,
satyrs and learned old women, broken busts,
past a fountain and tombstone
in the boxwood of our curious minds
that like the pole beans on the fence
expand perceptibly in the long rain.

Neurotic in July

Even desks and tables have edges sharp
as the blade of a guillotine today.
The wind gnashes its teeth in the oaks.
The translucent pearl fog of morning
is tarnished with my fear. One friend
dies at home in whatever pitted dignity
pain allows. Another friend lies dying
while the doctors in the hall mumble
their lies unsanctified as white lab rats.
Another comes out of a coma that almost
killed him, mischance exploding in the hands,
while in high glittery summer out on Route 6
tourists try to drive through each other's
bodies. The rescue squad drags their fatigue
to the third accident today, broken
glass and broken organs, the stench
of spilled gas and blood.

I jerk with anxiety, the reflexes
of a severed tail. Straw and sleet I am.
My thoughts spill, the contents of a dash
board ashtray, butts, roaches, seeds,

cores, bottlecaps. What I dream stinks.
Only in political rage can I scorn danger.
In daily life I quiver like a mass of frog's
eggs. Quaking I carry my breasts before
me like ripe figs a thumb could bruise
and, *Be careful! Be careful!* I croon
all day like a demented cuckoo with only
one harsh plaintive cry to those I love.

They pay no attention at all but wander
freely in and out of danger like sanderlings
feeding on the edge of the ocean as the tide
changes, chasing after each wave as it recedes,
racing before as the wave rushes back.

Attack of the squash people

And thus the people every year
in the valley of humid July
did sacrifice themselves
to the long green phallic god
and eat and eat and eat.

They're coming, they're on us,
the long striped gourds, the silky
babies, the hairy adolescents,
the lumpy vast adults
like the trunks of green elephants.
Recite fifty zucchini recipes!

Zucchini tempura; creamed soup;
sauté with olive oil and cumin,
tomatoes, onion; frittata;
casserole of lamb; baked
topped by cheese; marinated;
stuffed; stewed; driven
through the heart like a stake.

Get rid of old friends: they too
have gardens and full trunks.
Look for newcomers: befriend
them in the post office, unload
on them and run. Stop tourists

in the street. Take truckloads
to Boston. Give to your Red Cross.
Beg on the high roads: please
take my zucchini, I have a crippled
mother at home with heartburn.

Sneak out before dawn to drop
them in other people's gardens,
in baby buggies at churchdoors.
Shot, smuggling zucchini into
mailboxes, a federal offense.

With a suave reptilian glitter
you bask among your raspy
fronds sudden and huge as
alligators. You give and give
too much, like summer days
limp with heat, thunderstorms
bursting their bags on our heads,
as we salt and freeze and pickle
for the too little to come.

The inquisition

Did you love him? you stab the old
photographs. And him? And him? And her?
Oh, you shrug then. What does it mean?
Your love comes round regularly as the truck
that sweeps the streets, welcome but
hardly monumental. It stirs up the dust,
it goes on its way, doing some kind
of temporary good, busy, truculent.

You were only eight years old then, I say,
how could I love you if I'd been mean
and proper, if I'd rationed myself
like some prescription drug, if I'd frozen
on grit at the core waiting for the perfect
sun to melt me. I'm a survivor, a scavenger
and I make the best I can out of the daily
disaster, I mold my icons out of newspaper mâché.

How could you make love to him in an elevator
you say. But it was a freight elevator
I say, it went up very slowly, you could lock
it between floors. Besides that was a decade
ago, I was more adventurist then. Oh, you say,
so you wouldn't fuck me in an elevator, I see.
I like my comfort better now, I say, but you
are my only comfort. Have you an elevator in mind?

Look at this book, you say, you wrote him
twenty-two love poems. How could you? And publish
them. They weren't all to him, I say, I was busy

that year. And they're good, aren't they? Still?
Oh, so it's just literature, the ones you write
me. Words. But I write the truth out of my life
and if some truths are truer than others in
the long run, the short sprint makes poems too.

Listen, you idiot, we're crawling up the far
slope of our third year and still sometimes
I weep after we make love. It is love we make
and it feeds me daily like a good cow.
I'm an old tart and you come late and I have
loyalties scattered over the landscape like lots
I bought and pay taxes on still, but it's you
and Robert I live with, live in, live by.

Because we work together we are obscurely
joined deep in the soil, deep in the water
table where the pure vulnerable stream
flows in the dark sustaining all life. In dreams
you walk in my head arguing, we gallop
on thornapple quests, we lie in each other's
arms. What a richly colored strong warm coat
is woven when love is the warp and work is the woof.

Arofa

My little carry-on baggage,
my howler monkey, my blue-
eyed sleek beige passion,
you want a monogamous relationship
with me. Othella, if you were
big as me you'd have nipped
my head off in a fit.
Gourmet, winebibber, you fancy
a good Bordeaux as much
as schlag, but would rather
be petted than eat.
You play Ivan the Terrible
to guests, you hiss and slap
at them to go away. Only
an occasional lover gains
your tolerance if my smell
rubs off on him and he
lets you sleep in the bed.

When I travel you hurtle
about upending the rugs.
When I return you run from me.
Not till I climb into bed
are you content and crouch
between my breasts kneading,
a calliope of purrs.

When I got a kitten a decade
and a half ago, I didn't know
I was being acquired
by such a demanding lover,
such a passionate, jealous,
furry, fussy wife.

Cho-Cho

At the Animal Disposal League
you reached through the bars
avid to live. Discarded offspring
of Persian splendor and tuxedo
alley cat, your hunger saved
you, fuzzy and fist-sized.

Now you are sunny, opaque,
utterly beyond words, alien
as the dreams of a pine tree.
Sometimes when I look at you
you purr as if stroked.
Outside you turn your head
pretending not to see me
off on business, a rabbit
in the marshgrass, rendezvous
in the briars. In the house
you're a sponge for love,
a recirculating fountain.

Angry, you sulk way under
a bed till dragged out whining,
you permit yourself to be
captured and saved. You blink
then your goldengreen eyes
purr and collapse on your back

with paws up and your snowy
white belly exposed all curls
to the plume of your tail.
Ravish me, you say, with kisses
and tunafish because I know
how to accept pleasure. I am
your happy longhaired
id, taking the moment as I
do your finger in my mouth
without breaking its skin,
or eviscerating it instantly
like a mouse.

Cats like angels

Cats like angels are supposed to be thin;
pigs like cherubs are supposed to be fat.
People are mostly in between, a knob
of bone sticking out in the knee you might
like to pad, a dollop of flab hanging
over the belt. You punish yourself,
one of those rubber balls kids have
that come bouncing back off their own
paddles, rebounding on the same slab.
You want to be slender and seamless
as a bolt.
        When I was a girl
I loved spiny men with ascetic grimaces
all elbows and words and cartilage
ribbed like cast up fog-grey hulls,
faces to cut the eyes blind
on the glittering blade, chins
of Aegean prows bent on piracy.

Now I look for men whose easy bellies
show a love for the flesh and the table,
men who will come in the kitchen
and sit, who don't think peeling potatoes
makes their penis shrink; men with broad
fingers and purple figgy balls,

men with rumpled furrows and the slightly
messed look at ease of beds recently
well used.
   We are not all supposed
to look like undernourished fourteen year
old boys, no matter what the fashions
ordain. You are built to pull a cart,
to lift a heavy load and bear it,
to haul up the long slope, and so
am I, peasant bodies, earthy, solid
shapely dark glazed clay pots that can
stand on the fire. When we put our
bellies together we do not clatter
but bounce on the good upholstery.

A new constellation

We go intertwined, him and you
and me, her and him, you and her,
each the center of our own circle
of attraction and compulsion and gravity.
What a constellation we make: I call it
the Matrix. I call it the dancing
family. I call it wheels inside wheels.
Ezekiel did not know he was seeing
the pattern for enduring relationship
in the late twentieth century.

All the rings shine gold as wedding bands
but they are the hoops magicians use
that seem solid and unbroken, yet can slip
into chains of other rings and out.
They are strong enough to hang houses on,
strong enough to serve as cranes, yet
they are open. We fall through each other,
we catch each other, we cling, we flip on.

No one is at the center, but each
is her own center, no one controls
the jangling swing and bounce and merry-
go-round lurching intertangle of this mobile.
We pass through each other trembling

and we pass through each other shrieking
and we pass through each other shimmering.
The circle is neither unbroken
nor broken but living, a molecule attracting
atoms that wants to be a protein,
complex, mortal, able to sustain life,
able to reproduce itself inexactly,
learn and grow.

Indian pipe

Fragile drooped heads
white as rag paper
raise their funereal grace
ghostly on blanched needles,
year old tattered oak leaves.

The jointed stems suggest
the bones of marionettes.
Chill waxen flowers
blacken as they age
as if with fire.

Saprophytic poor relations
of wintergreen, surely
they embody decadence.

Yet decay is necessary
as the fox's lunge
bonded as we are
electron and proton,
eater and eaten. All
things have their uses
except morality
in the woods.

September afternoon
at four o'clock

Full in the hand, heavy
with ripeness, perfume spreading
its fan: moments now resemble
sweet russet pears glowing
on the bough, peaches warm
from the afternoon sun, amber
and juicy, flesh that can
make you drunk.

There is a turn in things
that makes the heart catch.
We are ripening, all the hard
green grasping, the stony will
swelling into sweetness, the acid
and sugar in balance, the sun
stored as energy that is pleasure
and pleasure that is energy.

Whatever happens, whatever,
we say, and hold hard and let
go and go on. In the perfect
moment the future coils,
a tree inside a pit. Take,
eat, we are each other's
perfection, the wine of our
mouths is sweet and heavy.
Soon enough comes the vinegar.
The fruit is ripe for the taking
and we take. There is
no other wisdom.

Morning athletes

for Gloria Nardin Watts

Most mornings we go running side by side
two women in mid-lives jogging, awkward
in our baggy improvisations, two
bundles of rejects from the thrift shop.
Men in their zippy outfits run in packs
on the road where we park, meet
like lovers on the wood's edge and walk
sedately around the corner out of sight
to our own hardened clay road, High Toss.

Slowly we shuffle, serious, panting
but talking as we trot, our old honorable
wounds in knee and back and ankle paining
us, short, fleshy, dark haired, Italian
and Jew, with our full breasts carefully
confined. We are rich earthy cooks
both of us and the flesh we are working
off was put on with grave pleasure. We
appreciate each other's cooking, each
other's art, photographer and poet, jogging
in the chill and wet and green, in the blaze
of young sun, talking over our work,
our plans, our men, our ideas, watching
each other like a pot that might boil dry
for that sign of too harsh fatigue.

It is not the running I love, thump
thump with my leaden feet that only
infrequently are winged and prancing,
but the light that glints off the cattails
as the wind furrows them, the rum cherries
reddening leaf and fruit, the way the pines
blacken the sunlight on their bristles,
the hawk flapping three times, then floating
low over beige grasses,
                              and your company
as we trot, two friendly dogs leaving
tracks in the sand. The geese call
on the river wandering lost in sedges
and we talk and pant, pant and talk
in the morning early and busy together.

The purge

Beware institutions begun with a purge,
beware buildings that require the bones
of a victim under the cornerstone, beware
undertakings launched with a blood
sacrifice, watch out for marriages
that start with a divorce.

To break a champagne bottle over the prow
of a boat is prodigal but harmless ; to break
a promise, a friendship much more exciting
(champagne doesn't squeal) ; but doesn't
the voyage require a lot of sightseeing
and loot to justify that splatter?

Give it up for me, she says, give him
up, give her up, look only in my eyes
and let me taste my power in their anguish.
How much do you love me? Let me count
the corpses as my cat brings home mangled
mice to arrange on my doormat like hors d'oeuvres.

But you know nobody dies of such executions.
Your discarded friends are drinking champagne
and singing off key just as if they were happy
without you. One person's garbage is another's
new interior decorating scheme. If she is your
whole world, how quickly the sun sets now.

Argiope

Your web spans a distance
of two of my hands spread
turning the space between unrelated
uprights, accidental neighbors, fennel, corn
stalks into a frame. The patterned web
startles me, as if a grasshopper
spoke, as if a moth whispered.
The bold design cannot have
a predatory use: no fly,
no mite or wasp caught by its zigzag
as my gaze is. Then I see you,
big, much bigger than I feel
spiders ought to be. Black and gold
you are a shiny brooch with legs
of derricks. I remind you
I am a general friend to your
kind. I rescue your kinfolk
from the bathtub fall mornings
before I run the water. I
remind you nervously we are
artisans, we both make out
of what we take in and what
we pass through our guts a patterned
object slung on the world.
I detour your net carefully

picking my way through the
pumpkin vines. The mother
of nightmares fatal and hungry,
you kill for a living. Beauty
is only a sideline, and your mate
approaches you with infinite
caution or you eat him too.
You stare at me, you do not
scuttle or hide, you wait.
I go round and leave you mistress
of your territory, not in
kindness but in awe. Stay
out of my dreams, Hecate
of the garden patch, Argiope.

From the tool and die shop

All right, using myself like the eggs,
the butter, the flour measured out
for a cake that in no way recalls
the modest piles from which its golden
sponge was assembled, is my pain
only raw ingredient?

If aches are wrought into artifact,
if spilled blood is read for omens
and my outcries are carefully shaped
for perusal, do I hurt less?
Probably. The effort distracts.
Is art a better aspirin?

The worm decorates its burrows
in tidal silt with bits of shell.
My cat sits washing her fur, arranging
each hair. If she misses a leap,
she pretends she meant to. Art is
part apology, part artifice, part act.

I writhe in pain, bellow want, purr
my sensual ease while the richest part
of what I touched sticks to my fingers.
Words say more than they mean. The poems
turn toward you out of my dirt and the best
know far more than I, far more than me.

For the young who want to

Talent is what they say
you have after the novel
is published and favorably
reviewed. Beforehand what
you have is a tedious
delusion, a hobby like knitting.

Work is what you have done
after the play is produced
and the audience claps.
Before that friends keep asking
when you are planning to go
out and get a job.

Genius is what they know you
had after the third volume
of remarkable poems. Earlier
they accuse you of withdrawing,
ask why you don't have a baby,
call you a bum.

The reason people want M.F.A.'s,
take workshops with fancy names
when all you can really
learn is a few techniques,

typing instructions and some-
body else's mannerisms

is that every artist lacks
a license to hang on the wall
like your optician, your vet
proving you may be a clumsy sadist
whose fillings fall into the stew
but you're certified a dentist.

The real writer is one
who really writes. Talent
is an invention like phlogiston
after the fact of fire.
Work is its own cure. You have to
like it better than being loved.

Memo to: Alta, Margaret Atwood, Olga Broumas, Diane
DiPrima, Miriam Dyak, Judy Grahn, Susan Griffin, June Jordan,
Faye Kicknosway, Maxine Kumin, Denise Levertov, Karen Lindsey,
Audre Lorde, Mary Mackey, Honor Moore, Robin Morgan,
Adrienne Rich, Sonia Sanchez, Kathleen Spivack, Alice Walker,
and all the rest of us female poets

Subject: Alternatives to what has become expected

When living resembles airport food;
when the morning paper hands you Chile
with the throat slit; the black children of South
Africa wounded thrashing like fish in a basket,
blood on asphalt the sun dries; when your last lover
announces her conversion to the Reverend Moon
explaining how your impure body impeded her pure mind;
when the second to last lover publishes
his novel in which you sprawl with your legs
spread saying all those things he always
wanted you to say, garish scenes you will have
to live with as if you had lived them
like a candid snap of you
on the toilet for the next twenty years;
when your daughter elopes with an FBI accountant
stealing your only credit card; when your son
shoots sugar and shit; when disdain
mounts you on a colored toothpick

like a smoked clam; when your friends misunderstand
your books and your enemies
understand them far too well;
when you lie alone on the sharp stones of unspoken
retorts fallen in the ravine of garrulous night
in the canyon of echoes where the dead
whisper reproaches; when you are empty of words,
a worm in your own apple,
ignore, ignore that death murmuring at your ear
like a lover far too pretty for you, whose attentions
flatter you, and how people will talk,
you will show them yet if you
but turn your head. Ignore those soft
shapes from the stone cold fog
welling from the back of the throat.

He is not pretty, that boy, only well
advertised. Give your enemies nothing.
Let our tears freeze to stones
we can throw from catapults.
Death is their mercenary, their agent.
He seduces you for hire.
After your death he will pander
your books and explain you.

I know we can't make promises.
Every work pushed out through the jagged
bottleneck sewer of the industry
is a defeat, mutilated before it's born.
My faucets drip at night too. I wake

tired. From the ceiling over my bed
troubles spin down on growing threads.
Only promise if you do get too weary,
take a bank president to lunch,
take a Rockefeller with you. Write
your own epitaph and say it loud.
This life is a war we are not yet
winning for our daughters' children.
Don't do your enemies' work for them.
Finish your own.

THE LUNAR CYCLE

The moon is always female

The moon is always female and so
am I although often in this vale
of razorblades I have wished I could
put on and take off my sex like a dress
and why not? Do men wear their sex
always? The priest, the doctor, the teacher
all tell us they come to their professions
neuter as clams and the truth is
when I work I am pure as an angel
tiger and clear is my eye and hot
my brain and silent all the whining
grunting piglets of the appetites.
For we were priests to the goddesses
to whom were fashioned the first altars
of clumsy stone on stone and leaping animal
in the wombdark caves, long before men
put on skirts and masks to scare babies.
For we were healers with herbs and poultices
with our milk and careful fingers
long before they began learning to cut up
the living by making jokes at corpses.
For we were making sounds from our throats
and lips to warn and encourage the helpless
young long before schools were built
to teach boys to obey and be bored and kill.

I wake in a strange slack empty bed
of a motel, shaking like dry leaves
the wind rips loose, and in my head
is bound a girl of twelve whose female
organs all but the numb womb are being

cut from her with a knife. Clitoridectomy,
whatever Latin name you call it, in a quarter
of the world girl children are so maimed
and I think of her and I cannot stop.
And I think of her and I cannot stop.

If you are a woman you feel the knife in the words.
If you are a man, then at age four or else
at twelve you are seized and held down
and your penis is cut off. You are left
your testicles but they are sewed to your
crotch. When your spouse buys you, you
are torn or cut open so that your precious
semen can be siphoned out, but of course
you feel nothing. But pain. But pain.

For the uses of men we have been butchered
and crippled and shut up and carved open
under the moon that swells and shines
and shrinks again into nothingness, pregnant
and then waning toward its little monthly
death. The moon is always female but the sun
is female only in lands where females
are let into the sun to run and climb.

A woman is screaming and I hear her.
A woman is bleeding and I see her
bleeding from the mouth, the womb, the breasts
in a fountain of dark blood of dismal
daily tedious sorrow quite palatable

to the taste of the mighty and taken for granted
that the bread of domesticity be baked
of our flesh, that the hearth be built
of our bones of animals kept for meat and milk,
that we open and lie under and weep.
I want to say over the names of my mothers
like the stones of a path I am climbing
rock by slippery rock into the mists.
Never even at knife point have I wanted
or been willing to be or become a man.
I want only to be myself and free.

I am waiting for the moon to rise. Here
I squat, the whole country with its steel
mills and its coal mines and its prisons
at my back and the continent tilting
up into mountains and torn by shining lakes
all behind me on this scythe of straw,
a sand bar cast on the ocean waves, and I
wait for the moon to rise red and heavy
in my eyes. Chilled, cranky, fearful
in the dark I wait and I am all the time
climbing slippery rocks in a mist while
far below the waves crash in the sea caves;
I am descending a stairway under the groaning
sea while the black waters buffet me
like rockweed to and fro.

I have swum the upper waters leaping
in dolphin's skin for joy equally into the nec-

essary air and the tumult of the powerful wave.
I am entering the chambers I have visited.
I have floated through them sleeping and sleep-
walking and waking, drowning in passion
festooned with green bladderwrack of misery.
I have wandered these chambers in the rock
where the moon freezes the air and all hair
is black or silver. Now I will tell you
what I have learned lying under the moon
naked as women do: now I will tell you
the changes of the high and lower moon.
Out of necessity's hard stones we suck
what water we can and so we have survived,
women born of women. There is knowing
with the teeth as well as knowing with
the tongue and knowing with the fingertips
as well as knowing with words and with all
the fine flickering hungers of the brain.

Right to life

SAILLE

A woman is not a pear tree
thrusting her fruit in mindless fecundity
into the world. Even pear trees bear
heavily one year and rest and grow the next.
An orchard gone wild drops few warm rotting
fruit in the grass but the trees stretch
high and wiry gifting the birds forty
feet up among inch long thorns
broken atavistically from the smooth wood.

A woman is not a basket you place
your buns in to keep them warm. Not a brood
hen you can slip duck eggs under.
Not the purse holding the coins of your
descendants till you spend them in wars.
Not a bank where your genes gather interest
and interesting mutations in the tainted
rain, any more than you are.

You plant corn and you harvest
it to eat or sell. You put the lamb
in the pasture to fatten and haul it in
to butcher for chops. You slice
the mountain in two for a road and gouge
the high plains for coal and the waters
run muddy for miles and years.
Fish die but you do not call them yours
unless you wished to eat them.

Now you legislate mineral rights in a woman.
You lay claim to her pastures for grazing,

fields for growing babies like iceberg
lettuce. You value children so dearly
that none ever go hungry, none weep
with no one to tend them when mothers
work, none lack fresh fruit,
none chew lead or cough to death and your
orphanages are empty. Every noon the best
restaurants serve poor children steaks.

At this moment at nine o'clock a *partera*
is performing a table top abortion on an
unwed mother in Texas who can't get Medicaid
any longer. In five days she will die
of tetanus and her little daughter will cry
and be taken away. Next door a husband
and wife are sticking pins in the son
they did not want. They will explain
for hours how wicked he is,
how he wants discipline.

We are all born of woman, in the rose
of the womb we suckled our mother's blood
and every baby born has a right to love
like a seedling to sun. Every baby born
unloved, unwanted is a bill that will come

due in twenty years with interest, an anger
that must find a target, a pain that will
beget pain. A decade downstream a child
screams, a woman falls, a synagogue is torched,
a firing squad is summoned, a button
is pushed and the world burns.

I will choose what enters me, what becomes
flesh of my flesh. Without choice, no politics,
no ethics lives. I am not your cornfield,
not your uranium mine, not your calf
for fattening, not your cow for milking.
You may not use me as your factory.
Priests and legislators do not hold
shares in my womb or my mind.
This is my body. If I give it to you
I want it back. My life
is a non-negotiable demand.

May apple

UATH

Hawthorn: spines long as my little finger
that glint in the sun before the leaves come out,
small white flowers like the wild rose
and fruits people don't eat. Virginity.

Not the hymen it took a week to drill through.
All at sixteen I could concentrate on
was what happened how and would it soon
while my mind turned into chewed bubblegum
and my periods racked me like earthquakes.

No, virginity in the old sense of a woman
unmated and not mating: solitude. A state
I have passed in and out of, the nature
of the dreaming mind nobody courts.

State of my cats when they are neither
in heat nor pregnant but predators, players,
brooding elegant gods. Sitting paws folded
and facing they blink courteously
and contemplate mathematical laws.

Eyes alter us by their observant gaze.
We are never the same after someone
has first loved us. The self the other
sees hangs in the mirror at least part time.

The innocence lost is living for myself,
ignorant as a wild hawthorn how to allure,

flatter, please and in what light arrange
the hair and limbs like a bouquet of white
flowers, dark twigs snipped off the tree.

Alone I am clear as clean ice.
I sleep short hours, stop cooking sauces,
and every day like a desert monk I contemplate
death in each apple core and woodash.

Alone I am twelve years old and eighty.
Alone I am sexless as a pine board.
Alone I am invisible to myself as carbon
dioxide. I touch myself often and then less
as my dreams darken into stained glass allegories.

Alone I find old fears preserved like hiking
boots at the bottom of the closet in a box,
my feet having shaped them just perfect to fit
and eight years later I set off in them to climb.

I become nocturnal. My eyes glow in the dark.
The moist rich parts of me contract underground
into tubers. What stands up still is strong
but crotchety, the village witch people come to
with savory troubles, all ears and teeth.

Shadows of the burning

DUIR

Oak burns steady and hot and long
and fires of oak are traditional tonight
but we light a fire of pitch pine
which burns well enough in the salt wind
whistling while ragged flames lick the dark
casting our shadows high as the dunes.

Come into the fire and catch,
come in, come in. Fire that burns
and leaves entire, the silver flame
of the moon, trembling mercury laying
on the waves a highway to the abyss,
the full roaring furnace of the sun at zenith
of the year and potency, midsummer's eve.

Come dance in the fire, come in.
This is the briefest night and just
under the ocean the fires of the sun
roll toward us. Already your skin is dark,
already your wiry curls are tipped with gold
and my black hair begins to redden.

How often I have leapt into that fire,
how often burned like a torch, my hair
streaming sparks, and wakened to weep
ashes. I have said, love is a downer we take,
love is a habit like sucking on death tit cigarettes,
love is a bastard art. Instead of painting
or composing, we compose a beloved.
When you love for a living, I have said,
you're doomed to early retirement without benefits.

For women have died and worms have eaten them
and just for love. Love of the wrong man or
the right. Death from abortion, from the first
child or the eighteenth, death at the stake
for loving a woman or freedom or the wrong
deity. Death at the open end of a gun
from a jealous man, a vengeful man,
Othello's fingers, Henry's ax.

It is romance I loathe, the swooning moon
of June which croons to the tune of every goon.
Venus on the half shell without the reek
of seaweed preferred to Artemis of the rows
of breasts like a sow and the bow
ready in her hand that kills and the herbs
that save in childbirth.

Ah, my name hung once like a can
on an ink stained girl blue as skim milk
lumpy with elbows, spiky with scruples,
who knelt in a tower raised of Shelley's bones
praying my demon lover asceticism
to grant one icy vision.

I found my body in the arms of lovers
and woke in the flesh alive, astounded
like a corpse sitting up in a judgment
day painting. My own five hound senses
turned on me, chased me, tore me
head from trunk. Thumb and liver

and jaw on the bloody hillside
twanged like frogs in the night I am alive!

A succession of lovers like a committee
of Congress in slow motion put me back
together, a thumb under my ear, the ear
in an armpit, the head sprouting feet.
Kaleidoscope where glass sparks pierced
my eyes, in love's funhouse I was hung
a mirror of flesh reflecting flaccid ideas
of men scouting their mothers through my womb,
a labyrinth of years in other
people's thoroughly furnished rooms.

I built myself like a house a poor family
puts up in the country: first the foundation
under a tarred flat roof like a dugout,
then the well in the spring and you get
electricity connected and maybe the next
fall you seal in two rooms and add some
plumbing but all the time you're living
there constructing your way out of a slum.
Yet for whom is this built if not to be shared
with the quick steps and low voice of love?

I cherish friendship and loving that starts
in liking but the body is the church
where I praise and bless and am blessed.
My strength and my weakness are twins

in the same womb, mirrored dancers under
water, the dark and light side of the moon.
I know how truly my seasons have turned
cold and hot
around that lion-bodied sun.

Come step into the fire, come in,
come in, dance in the flames of the festival
of the strongest sun at the mountain top
of the year when the wheel starts down.
Dance through me as I through you.
Here in the heart of fire in the caves
of the ancient body we are aligned
with the stars wheeling, the midges swarming
in the humid air like a nebula, with the clams
who drink the tide and the heartwood clock
of the oak and the astronomical clock
in the blood thundering through the great heart
of the albatross. Our cells are burning
each a little furnace powered by the sun
and the moon pulls the sea of our blood.
This night the sun and moon dance
and you and I dance in the fire of which
we are the logs, the matches and the flames.

The sabbath of mutual respect

TINNE

In the natural year come two thanksgivings,
the harvest of summer and the harvest of fall,
two times when we eat and drink and remember our dead
under the golden basin of the moon of plenty.

Abundance, Habondia, food for the winter,
too much now and survival later. After
the plant bears, it dies into seed.
The blowing grasses nourish us, wheat
and corn and rye, millet and rice, oat
and barley and buckwheat, all the serviceable
grasses of the pasture that the cow grazes,
the lamb, the horse, the goat; the grasses
that quicken into meat and milk and cheese,
the humble necessary mute vegetable bees,
the armies of the grasses waving their
golden banners of ripe seed.
                              The sensual
round fruit that gleams with the sun
stored in its sweetness.
                              The succulent
ephemera of the summer garden, bloodwarm
tomatoes, tender small squash, crisp
beans, the milky corn, the red peppers
exploding like roman candles in the mouth.

We praise abundance by eating of it,
reveling in choice on a table set with roses
and lilies and phlox, zucchini and lettuce

and eggplant before the long winter
of root crops.
                    Fertility and choice:
every row dug in spring means weeks
of labor. Plant too much and the seedlings
choke in weeds as the warm rain soaks them.
The goddess of abundance Habondia is also
the spirit of labor and choice.
                    In another
life, dear sister, I too would bear six fat
children. In another life, my sister, I too
would love another woman and raise one child
together as if that pushed from both our wombs.
In another life, sister, I too would dwell
solitary and splendid as a lighthouse on the rocks
or be born to mate for life like the faithful goose.
Praise all our choices. Praise any woman
who chooses, and make safe her choice.

Habondia, Artemis, Cybele, Demeter, Ishtar,
Aphrodite, Au Set, Hecate, Themis, Lilith,
Thea, Gaia, Bridgit, The Great Grandmother of Us
All, Yemanja, Cerridwen, Freya, Corn Maiden,
Mawu, Amaterasu, Maires, Nut, Spider-Woman,
Neith, Au Zit, Hathor, Inanna, Shin Moo,
Diti, Arinna, Anath, Tiamat, Astoreth:
the names flesh out our histories, our choices,
our passions and what we will never embody
but pass by with respect. When I consecrate

my body in the temple of our history,
when I pledge myself to remain empty
and clear for the voices coming through
I do not choose for you or lessen your choice.

Habondia, the real abundance, is the power
to say yes and to say no, to open
and to close, to take or to leave
and not to be taken by force or law
or fear or poverty or hunger or need.
To bear children or not to bear by choice
is holy. To bear children unwanted
is to be used like a public sewer.
To be sterilized unchosen is to have
your heart cut out. To love women
is holy and holy is the free love of men
and precious to live taking whichever comes
and precious to live unmated as a peachtree.
Praise the lives you did not choose.
They will heal you, tell your story, fight
for you. You eat the bread of their labor.
You drink the wine of their joy. I tell you
after I went under the surgeon's knife
for the laparoscopy I felt like a trumpet
an Amazon was blowing sonorous charges on.
Then my womb learned to open on the full
moon without pain and my pleasure deepened
till my body shuddered like troubled water.
When my friend gave birth I held her in joy
as the child's head thrust from her vagina
like the sun rising at dawn wet and red.

Praise our choices, sisters, for each doorway
open to us was taken by squads of fighting
women who paid years of trouble and struggle,
who paid their wombs, their sleep, their lives
that we might walk through these gates upright.
Doorways are sacred to women for we
are the doorways of life and we must choose
what comes in and what goes out. Freedom
is our real abundance.

Tumbling and with tangled mane

COLL

1.

I wade in milk.
Only beige sand exists as the floor
of a slender nave before me.
Mewing fishhook cries of gulls
pierce the white from what must be up.
The fog slides over me like a trained
snake leaving salt on my lips. Somewhere
I can hear the ocean breathing.
The world is a benign jellyfish.
I float inhaling water that tastes
of iodine and thin bright blood.

2.

We squat on a sandbar digging as the tide
turns and runs to bury the crosshatched scales,
the ribs of the bottom as if the ebbing
of waters exposed that the world is really
a giant flounder. As we wade landward
the inrushing tide is so cold
my ankles ring like glass bells.
We lie belly up baking as the ocean
ambles toward us nibbling the sand.
Out to sea a fog bank stands like world's
end, the sharp place where boats fall off.

3.

When a storm halts, people get into their
cars. They don't start picking up yet, the bough
that crashed on the terrace, the window
shattered. No, they rush with foot hard down
on the accelerator over the wet winding black
topped roads where the pine and oak start out
normal size and get smaller till they are
forests for mice. Cars line up on the bluff
facing waves standing tall as King Kong,
skyscrapers smashed before a giant wrecking ball.
Mad water avalanches. You can't hear.
Your hair fills with wet sand. Your windshield
is being sandblasted and will blind you as the sun
burns a hole in the mist like a cigarette
through a tablecloth and sets fire to the air.

4.

A dream, two hundred times the same. The shore
can be red rocks, black or grey, sand dunes
or barrier reef. The sun blazes. The sky
roars a hard blue, blue as policemen.
The water is kicking. The waves leap
at the shore like flames out of control.
The sea gnashes snow capped mountains

that hurl themselves end over end, blocking
the sky. A tidal wave eats the land. Rearing
and galloping, tumbling and with tangled
mane the horses of the surf with mad eyes,
with snorting nostrils and rattling hooves
stampede at the land. I am in danger
yet I do not run. I am rooted watching
knowing that what I watch
is also me.

Making makes guilt. Cold fierce mother
who gouges deep into this pamet, who
rests her dragon's belly on the first rocks,
older than land, older than memory,
older than life, my power is so little
it makes me laugh how in my dreaming
lemur's mind making poems or tales or re-
volution is this storm on a clear day.

Of course danger and power mingle in all
birthing. We die by what we live by.
Again and again that dream comes when I set
off journeying to the back of my mind,
the bottom of the library, a joust with
what is : the sun a fiery spider high
overhead, the colors bright and clear as glass,
the sea raging at the coast, always about

to overrun it, as in the eye of a hurricane
when the waves roll cascading in undiminished
but for a moment and in that place the air
is still, the moment of clarity out
of time at the center of an act.

Cutting the grapes free

MUIN

In spring the vine looks like a crucified
witch tied hard to high wires strung
from weathered posts. Those shaggy tormented
limbs shall never flow with sap,
dry as bones the ants have polished,
inert, resistant as obsidian.

Then from the first velvet buds tearing
open the wands stretch bouquets of skinny
serpents coiling along the wires to bury
them in rampant swelling leaves, a dense
fluttering cascade of heavy green over
the trellis and path, climbing the pine.

Now the grapes swell in the sun yellow
and black and ruby mounds of breast
and testicle, the image of ripe flesh
rounding warm to the fingers. The wasps
and bees drone drunken, our lips, our
tongues stained purple with juice, and sweet.

We bleed when we blossom from the straight
grainy pine of girlhood. We bleed when we taste
first of men. We bleed when we bear and when
we don't. Vine, from my blood is fermented
poetry and from yours wine that tunes my sinews
and nerves till they sing instead of screeching.

I do not seek immortality, to be a rock
which only dissolves in slow motion,
but to age well like good wine harsh young
but fit to lay down, the best of me
in the dark of libraries and minds to be taken
with care into the light and savored.

I do not seek to leap free from the wheel
of change but to dance in that turning.
What depends more on the seasons
and the years than wine: whether rains come,
the pounding hail, the searing drought,
the lethal hoar kiss of the frost?

In this glass the Mosel pale as straw
shines with the sun of a spent year
and pricks my tongue with tiny bubbles
that were not in it last week. The vines
of its home are blossoming and the wine
remembers its natal soil as I must.

The press of the years bears down
on us till we bleed from every pore
yet in our cells sun is stored in honey
ready to be spilled or to nurture.
Like wine I must finally trust myself
to other tongues or turn to vinegar.

The perpetual migration

GORT

How do we know where we are going?
How do we know where we are headed
till we in fact or hope or hunch
arrive? You can only criticize,
the comfortable say, you don't know
what you want. Ah, but we do.

We have swung in the green verandas
of the jungle trees. We have squatted
on cloud-grey granite hillsides where
every leaf drips. We have crossed
badlands where the sun is sharp as flint.
We have paddled into the tall dark sea
in canoes. We always knew.

Peace, plenty, the gentle wallow
of intimacy, a bit of Saturday night
and not too much Monday morning,
a chance to choose, a chance to grow,
the power to say no and yes, pretties
and dignity, an occasional jolt of truth.

The human brain, wrinkled slug, knows
like a computer, like a violinist, like
a bloodhound, like a frog. We remember
backwards a little and sometimes forwards,
but mostly we think in the ebbing circles
a rock makes on the water.

The salmon hurtling upstream seeks
the taste of the waters of its birth
but the seabird on its four-thousand-mile
trek follows charts mapped on its genes.
The brightness, the angle, the sighting
of the stars shines in the brain luring
till inner constellation matches outer.

The stark black rocks, the island beaches
of waveworn pebbles where it will winter
look right to it. Months after it set
forth it says, home at last, and settles.
Even the pigeon beating its short whistling
wings knows the magnetic tug of arrival.

In my spine a tidal clock tilts and drips
and the moon pulls blood from my womb.
Driven as a migrating falcon, I can be blown
off course yet if I turn back it feels
wrong. Navigating by chart and chance
and passion I will know the shape
of the mountains of freedom, I will know.

The great horned owl

I wake after midnight and hear
you hunting: that sound seems to lodge
in the nape like a hollow bullet,
a rhythmic hooting plaintive as if
you seduced your prey by pity.

How you swoop from the dark of the trees
against the blackest blue sky of the November
full moon, your wings spread wide as my
arms, rough heavy sails rigged for a storm.
The moon blinds me as she glides in ripping
skeins of cloud. On your forehead you bear
her crescents, your eyes hypnotic
as her clock-face disc. Gale force winds
strip crispened leaves from the branches
and try the strength of the wood. The weakest
die now, giving back their bodies
for the white sheet of the snow to cover.

Now my cats are not let out after sunset
because you own the night. After two years
you return to my land. I fear and protect
you, come to harry the weak in the long dark.
Pellets of mouse and bird and shrew bone
I will find at the base of the pines.
You have come to claim your nest again
in the old white oak whose heart is thick
with age, and in the dead of the winter
when the snow has wept into ice and frozen
and been buried again in snow and crusted over,

you will give birth before the willow buds
swell and all night you will hunt for those
first babies of the year, downy owlets shivering.
Waking to hear you I touch the warm back
of my lover sleeping beside me on his stomach
like a child.

The longest night

RUIS

The longest night is long drawn
as a freight blocking a grade crossing
in a prairie town when I am trying
to reach Kansas City to sleep and one
boxcar clatters after the other, after
and after in faded paint proclaiming
as they trundle through the headlights
names of 19th-century fortunes, scandals,
labor wars. Stalled between factory
and cemetery I lean on the cold wheel.
The factory is still, the machines
turned off; the cemetery looks boring
and factual as a parking lot. Too cold
for the dead to stir, tonight even
my own feel fragile as brown bags
carted to the dump. Ash stains the air.
Wheels of the freight clack by. Snow
hisses on the windshield of the rented car.
Always a storm at the winter solstice.

New moon, no moon, old moon dying,
moon that gives no light, stub
of a candle, dark lantern, face
without features, the zone of zero:
I feel the blood starting. Monthly
my womb opens on the full moon but
my body is off its rhythms. I am
jangled and raw. I do not celebrate

this blood seeping as from a wound.
I feel my weakness summoning me
like a bed of soft grey ashes
I might crawl into.

Here in the pit of the year scars overlap
scabs, the craters of the moon, stone
breaking stone. In the rearview mirror
my black hair fades into the night,
my cheeks look skeletal, my dark eyes,
holes a rat might hide in. I sense
death lurking up the road like a feral
dog abroad in the swirling snow.

Defeat, defeat, defeat, tedious
as modern headstones, regular as dentures.
My blood tastes salty as tears and rusty
as an old nail. Yet as I kick the car
over the icy tracks toward nowhere
I want to be, I am grinning. Lady, it's been
worse before, bad as the moon burning,
bad as the moon's horn goring my side,
that to give up now is a joke told
by the FBI minding the tap or the binoculars
staking me out on such a bitter night
when the blood slows and begins to freeze.
I grew up among these smoke-pitted houses
choking over the railroad between the factory

shuddering and the cemetery for the urban
poor, and I got out. They say that's
what you ask for. And how much more
I ask. To get everybody out.

Hecate, lady of the crossroads, vampires
of despair you loose and the twittering
bats of sleepless fear. The three-headed
dog barking in the snow obeys you.
Tonight I honor you, lady of last things.
Without you to goad me I would lie
late in the warm bed of the flesh.
The blood I coughed from my lungs that year
you stood at the foot of my bed was sour,
acrid, the taste of promises broken
and since then I have run twice as fast.
Your teeth are in me, like tiny headstones.
This moon is the void around which the serpent
with its tail in its mouth curls.
Where there is no color, no light,
no sound, what is? The dark of the mind.
In terror begins vision. In silence
I learn my song, here at the stone
nipple, the black moon bleeding,
the egg anonymous as water,
the night that goes on and on,
a tunnel through the earth.

At the well

BETH

Though I'm blind now and age
has gutted me to rubbing bones
knotted up in a leather sack
like Old Man Jacob I wrestled an angel.
It happened near that well by Peniel
where the water runs copper cold
even in drought. Sore and dusty
I was traveling my usual rounds
wary of strangers, for some men
think nothing of setting on any woman
alone, doctoring a bit, setting bones,
herbs and simples I know well,
divining for water with a switch,
selling my charms of odd shaped bones
and stones with fancy names to less
skeptical women wanting a lover, a son,
a husband, or relief from one.

The stones were sharp as shinbones under me.
When I woke up at midnight it had come,
not he, I thought, not she but a presence furious
as a goat about to butt.
Amused as those yellow eyes
sometimes seem just before the hind
legs kick hard.
The angel struck me
and we wrestled all that night.
My dust-stained gristle of a body
clad in proper village black
was pushed against him
and his fiery chest

fell through me like a star.
Raw with bruises, with my muscles
sawing like donkey's brays,
I thought fighting can be
making love. Then in the grey
placental dawn I saw.

"I know you now, face
on a tree of fire
with eyes of my youngest sweetest
dead, face
I saw in the mirror
right after my first child
was born—before it failed—
when I was beautiful.
Whatever you are, whatever
I've won a blessing
from you. Bless me!"

The angel, "Yes, we have met
at doors thrust open to an empty room,
a garden, or a pit.
My gifts have human faces
hieroglyphs that command
you without yielding what they mean.
Cast yourself
and I will bless your cast
till your bones are dice
for the wind to roll.
I am the demon of beginnings

for those who leap their thresholds
and let the doors swing shut."

My hair bristling, I stood.
"Get away from me, old
enemy. I know the lying
radiance of that face:
my friend, my twin, my
lover I trusted as the fish
the water, who left me
carrying his child.
The man who bought me
with his strength and beat
me for his weakness.
The girl I saved who turned
and sold her skin
for an easy bed in a house
of slaves. The boy fresh
as a willow sapling
smashed on the stones of war."

"I am the spirit of hinges,
the fever that lives in dice
and cards, what is picked
up and thrown down. I am
the new that is ancient,
the hope that hurts,
what begins in what has ended.
Mine is the double vision
that everything is sacred, and trivial,

the laughter that bubbles in blood,
and I love the blue beetle
clicking in the grass as much
as you. Shall I bless you
child and crone?"

"What has plucked the glossy
pride of hair from my scalp,
loosened my teeth in their sockets,
wrung my breasts dry as gullies,
rubbed ashes into my sleep
but chasing you?
Now I clutch a crust and I hold on.
Get from me
wielder of the heart's mirages.
I will follow you to no more graves."

I spat
and she gathered her tall shuddering wings
and scaled the streaks of the dawn
a hawk on fire soaring
and I stood there and could hear the water burbling
and raised my hand
before my face and groped:
Why has the sun gone out?
Why is it dark?

White on black

LUIS

They say the year begins in January, but it
feels like the same old year to me. Things
give out now, the cabbages rot, the rent
in the coat sleeve's too worn to be mended,
the boot finally admits it leaks, the candle
nub gutters out with a banner of pungent smoke.

The cracked dish of the frozen moon lights
the snow far longer than the old fox of the sun
that can hardly scale the hill, that crawls
feebly into the lower branches of the pine
and drops to earth exhausted.   Little sister
of the moon you prance on the ice with
delicate black feet. Your eyes shine red.
You comb your long tail and plume it out.
You mate under the porch. With sharp claws
you dig up the compost and scavenge the dump.
The air is crystal up to the ice splinters
of stars but you raise the quickest warm
nose in the woods, long, sharp as your hunger.

In the path you wait for me to give way.
Often you die bloody in the road because
you expect deference. The wise dog looks
the other way when you cross his yard.
The stupid dog never bothers you twice.

Little sister, mostly when we meet we bow
rather formally and go our ways, me
first. I read in a book that perhaps if one

lifted you by your tail, you could not spray
or perhaps you could. I envision a man
in a space suit lumbering over the plain
of the Herring River to catch and lift
you in the name of science. Then the space
suit would be burned perhaps or perhaps
not. My cats and I sit in the darkened
livingroom watching through the glass
as you dance and nibble, your long fur
sweeping the snow and your nailed feet quick.

Another country

NION

When I visited with the porpoises
I felt awkward, my hairy
angular body sprouting its skinny
grasping limbs like long mistakes.
The child of gravity and want I sank
in the salt wave clattering with gadgets,
appendages. Millennia past
they turned and fled back to the womb.
There they feel no fatigue but slip
through the water caressed and buoyed up.
Never do they sleep but their huge brains
hold life always turning it like a pebble
under the tongue, and lacking practice, death
comes as an astonishment.

In the wide murmur of the sea they fear
little. Together they ram the shark.
Food swims flashing in schools.
Hunger is only a teasing, endured
no longer than desired. Weather
is superficial decoration; they rise
to salute the thunder, romping their tails.

They ride through pleasure and plenty
secure in a vast courtesy
firm enough to sustain a drowning man.
Nothing is said bluntly.
All conversation is a singing,
all telling alludes to and embodies
minute displacements in epic,

counter-epic, comic opera, or the four hundred
forty-one other genres they recognize
as current. Every exchange comes
as aria, lyric, set piece, recitativo,
and even a cry for help is couched
in a form brief and terse,
strict as haiku.

Greed has no meaning when no one
is hungry. Thus they swim toward
us with broad grins and are slaughtered
by the factory ships
that harvest the tuna like wheat.

Crescent moon like a canoe

FEARN

This month you carried me late and heavy
in your belly and finally near Tuesday
midnight you gave me light and life, the season
Kore returns to Demeter, and you suffer
and I cannot save you though I burn with dreams.

Memories the color of old blood,
scraps of velvet gowns, lace, chiffon veils,
your sister's stage costumes (Ziegfeld
didn't stint) we lingered together, you
padding in sneakers and wash-worn housedresses.

You grew celery by tucking sliced off
bottoms in the soil. You kept a compost
pile in 1940. Your tomatoes glowed
like traffic signals in the table-sized yard.
Don't kill spiders, you warned.

In an asbestos box in Detroit where sputtering
factories yellow the air, where sheets
on the line turn ashen, you nurtured
a backyard jungle. Every hungry cat
wanted to enter and every child.

You who had not been allowed to finish
tenth grade but sent to be a frightened
chambermaid, carried home every week
armloads of books from the library
rummaging them late at night, insomniac,

riffling the books like boxes of chocolates
searching for the candied cherries, the nuts,

hunting for the secrets, the formulae,
the knowledge those others learned
that made them shine and never ache.

You were taught to feel stupid; you
were made to feel dirty; you were
forced to feel helpless; you were trained
to feel lost, uprooted, terrified.
You could not love yourself or me.

Dreamer of fables that hid their own
endings, kitchen witch, reader of palms,
you gave me gifts and took them back
but the real ones boil in the blood
and swell in the breasts, furtive, strong.

You gave me hands that can pick up
a wild bird so that the bird relaxes,
turns and stares. I have handled
fifty stunned and injured birds and killed
only two through clumsiness, with your touch.

You taught me to see the scale on the bird
leg, the old woman's scalp pink as a rose
under the fluff, the golden flecks in the iris
of your eye, the silver underside of leaves
blown back. I am your poet, mother.

You did not want the daughter you got.
You wanted a girl to flirt as you did
and marry as you had and chew the same

sour coughed up cud, yet you wanted too
to birth a witch, a revenger, a sword

of hearts who would do all the things
you feared. Don't do it, they'll kill
you, you're bad, you said, slapping me down
hard but always you whispered, I could have!
Only rebellion flashes like lightning.

I wanted to take you with me, you don't
remember. We fought like snakes, biting
hard at each other's spine to snap free.
You burned my paper armor, rifled my diaries,
snuffed my panties looking for smudge of sex,

so I took off and never came back. You can't
imagine how I still long to save you,
to carry you off, who can't trust me
to make coffee, but your life and mine pass
in different centuries, under altered suns.

I see your blood soaking into the linoleum,
I see you twisted, a mop some giant hand
is wringing out. Pain in the careless joke
and shouted insult and knotted fist. Pain like knives
and forks set out on the domestic table.

You look to men for salvation and every year
finds you more helpless. Do I battle
for other women, myself included,

because I can not give you anything
you want? I can not midwife you free.

In my childhood bed we float, your sweet
husky voice singing about the crescent
moon, with two horns sharp and bright we would
climb into like a boat and row away
and see, you sang, where the pretty moon goes.

In the land where the moon hides, mothers
and daughters hold each other tenderly.
There is no male law at five o'clock.
Our sameness and our difference do not clash
metal on metal but we celebrate and learn.

My muse, your voice on the phone wavers with tears.
The life you gave me burns its acetylene
of buried anger, unused talents, rotted wishes,
the compost of discontent, flaring into words
strong for other women under your waning moon.